The Goal Achiever's

Blueprint Series

Unlocking the 7 Key Traits to Success

Motivation
and Inspiration

M. Marcus Harris

The Goal Achiever's Blueprint: Unlocking the 7 The Goal Achiever's Blueprint: Unlocking the 7 Key Traits to Success—Motivation and Inspiration ©2024 M. Marcus Harris

Printed in the United States of America

First Edition

Photography by Pleasantly Captured Photography

Print ISBN: 978-1-68598-022-1

E-book ISBN: 978-1-68598-030-6

Write Womb Ink

To inquire about permissions, bulk sales, or any other queries, please email contact@marioharris.com.

The Visionary Mindset is the first book in the *Goal Achiever's Blueprint* series. For updates on upcoming book releases, visit www.marioharris.com

Goal Achiever's Blueprint Series

1. The Visionary Mindset
2. Embracing Resilience and Persistence
3. Strategic Planning
4. Motivation and Inspiration
5. Discipline and Consistency
6. Embracing Change and Overcoming Challenges
7. Building Strong Relationships

Dedication

It's my pleasure to say thank you to some of my mentors and fellow Marines: Mr. Nathaniel Alston (Mrs. Rose Alston), Deacon Isaiah "Ike" Johnson (Mama Johnson), Dr. Verlando "Lee" Frazier (Mrs. Pat), Mr. Maruice Black (Kim), Deacon Aaron West (Nannette), Mr. Eric Hollins (Kelly), Mr. Heath Martin, Pastor William Hayden Jr. (Anne), Mr. Errick Wells, Michael and Lisa McNeal, Ms. Kimberley Gray, Ms. Michelle Morris, Mr. Aldelaido Martinez, Mr. Keith Strand (Michelle), Mr. Jeffrey Barrett (Kim), Mr. Kevin Brooks Sr., and Minister Micheal Warren.

Contents

Foreword

In life, there are moments when the weight of our challenges seems unbearable and the road ahead feels unclear. It is in these moments that we must seek out the voices, stories, and wisdom that remind us of who we are and who we are destined to become.

The Goal Achiever's Blueprint Series: Book Four – Motivation and Inspiration stands as one of those voices. It is more than just a collection of words; it is a call to action, a guidepost for the soul, and a reminder that greatness is not reserved for the few, but available to anyone who dares to pursue it.

As someone who has witnessed the power of perseverance, faith, and discipline firsthand, I can tell you that motivation will get you started, but inspiration will keep you going. This book skillfully blends both. It provides practical lessons that encourage us to push past our comfort zones, and it ignites the internal spark we all possess to overcome adversity and achieve our personal best. The author has poured both heart and experience into these pages. Each chapter is crafted to challenge your thinking, encourage reflection, and offer real strategies for growth. Whether you are a student finding your path, a professional striving for the next level, or a leader charged with guiding others, this book speaks to you.

How should you apply it to your life? I encourage you to do more than just read it — study it, reflect on it, and most importantly, act on it. Let the principles within become part of your daily routine. Set meaningful goals, cultivate positive habits, and surround yourself with people who lift you higher. Allow this book to be your companion on the journey to becoming the best version of yourself.

Remember, true motivation and inspiration come from within, but the right words at the right time can change the trajectory of your life. *Book 4: Motivation and Inspiration* is that timely message. I hope that it touches your heart, sharpens your vision, and propels you into purposeful action.

Stay inspired. Stay motivated. Keep climbing.

Mr. Carl Green Sr.

Father, Grandfather, Scholar, Mentor, and Community Advocate

Introduction

Motivation and inspiration are key to achieving success. These powerful motivators ignite our passion and provide the energy to persevere through challenges. Investigating our inner motivations and inspirations requires a deeper understanding of ourselves and our ambitions. This understanding can help us stay focused, committed, and determined to achieve our goals when harnessed effectively.

Motivation is the inner drive that compels us to take action toward our goals. It can stem from various sources, such as personal values, past experiences, or future aspirations. When we are motivated, we are more likely to persist through obstacles, setbacks, and failures. Conversely, inspiration often comes from external sources such as role models, mentors, or success stories. It has the power to spark creativity, instill confidence, and broaden our perspective on what is possible.

By recognizing and embracing these sources of motivation and inspiration, we can cultivate a positive mindset that propels us toward success. Setting clear goals, creating a vision board, surrounding ourselves with supportive individuals, and engaging in activities that energize us are ways to nurture our motivation and inspiration.

By tapping into these sources of strength, we can elevate our performance, overcome challenges, and realize our full potential. Continually nurturing and cultivating these driving forces is essential to stay focused, committed, and resilient on our path to success.

Leading business coaches and speakers have delved into the topics of motivation and inspiration and how they influence personal and professional success. For instance, Tony Robbins, a well-known motivational speaker and coach, stresses that motivation is crucial for achieving success. According to Robbins, motivation stems from having a compelling vision, establishing clear goals, and discovering a profound sense of purpose. He stresses that focusing on the value of goal attainment and its associated emotional rewards can ignite inspiration.

Author and speaker, Simon Sinek advocates finding one's "why" as a source of motivation and inspiration. He suggests that understanding the purpose and values that drive our actions can ignite passion and create a sense of fulfillment. Sinek believes true motivation comes from aligning our actions with our core beliefs and values.

Motivational speaker, Mel Robbins, emphasizes the importance of taking action to generate motivation. She suggests that waiting for motivation to strike before acting is counterproductive and encourages individuals to use the "5 Second Rule." This rule involves taking action within five seconds of feeling the urge to do something, helping individuals overcome procrastination and generate momentum.

Motivational speaker Les Brown stresses positive mindsets for motivation and success. He advises people to seek positive influences, visualize success, and consistently work toward their goals.

Likewise, motivational speaker and author Lisa Nichols stresses the crucial role of self-belief in finding motivation and inspiration. She encourages people to change how they see themselves, recognize their value, and trust their potential for greatness.

As you can see, leading business coaches and speakers agree that motivation and inspiration are essential for achieving success. They emphasize the importance of having a compelling vision, setting clear goals, finding one's "why," taking action, cultivating a positive mindset, surrounding oneself with support, embracing personal growth, and believing in one's abilities.

On the following pages, you will discover how to harness the power of motivation and inspiration. This will help you overcome challenges, maintain resilience, and unlock your potential in personal and professional endeavors.

Intrinsic and Extrinsic Motivation: Unlocking the Power Within

Intrinsic motivation arises from within, while extrinsic motivation comes from external sources. Understanding both types, and how they influence behavior, allows for effective leverage to sustain drive and determination. This motivational force propels us toward goals and aspirations. Therefore, by effectively using both intrinsic and extrinsic motivation, we unlock our potential to achieve remarkable feats.

Understanding Intrinsic and Extrinsic Motivation

Intrinsic motivation stems from internal factors and personal desires. It is driven by a genuine interest in an activity or a deep sense of enjoyment and fulfillment derived from the task. Intrinsic motivation is fueled by internal rewards such as satisfaction, joy, personal growth, and a sense of mastery. It is often associated with activities that align with our passions, values, and strengths.

Extrinsic motivation, on the other hand, arises from external factors and rewards. It involves engaging in a task or activity to obtain external rewards or avoid punishment. Extrinsic motivation can come in various forms, such as money, recognition, praise, grades, or social status. While extrinsic motivation can provide short-term incentives, it is typically less sustainable and may not foster long-term satisfaction.

The Effects of Intrinsic Motivation

Understanding how intrinsic and extrinsic motivation work is crucial to using them effectively. Let's examine the effects of intrinsic motivation.

INCREASED ENJOYMENT AND ENGAGEMENT

Intrinsic motivation fosters a deep sense of enjoyment and engagement in an activity. When intrinsically motivated, we find satisfaction in the process, leading to heightened focus, creativity, and a willingness to invest time and effort into the task.

SUSTAINED EFFORT AND PERSEVERANCE

Intrinsic motivation provides the drive to persist and persevere, even when faced with challenges or setbacks. The inherent enjoyment and fulfillment derived from the task fuels our determination, allowing us to overcome obstacles and achieve long-term success.

GREATER AUTONOMY AND SELF-DETERMINATION

Intrinsic motivation gives us a sense of autonomy and control over our actions. When driven by internal factors, we feel a sense of choice and ownership in our tasks, contributing to fulfillment and satisfaction. For example, a writer who loves crafting stories and finds joy in the process itself is intrinsically motivated. Their motivation isn't money or fame; they write because the act of writing is rewarding in itself. The internal drive cultivates a deeper sense of involvement and satisfaction than writing solely to meet external deadlines or receive payment.

The Effects of Extrinsic Motivation

IMMEDIATE REWARDS AND INCENTIVES

Extrinsic motivation offers immediate rewards and incentives that can drive behavior and performance. The use of external motivators, such as monetary bonuses or public recognition for a job well done, can prove highly effective in the short term, driving us to take the necessary actions required to meet our specific targets and achieve short-term objectives.

COMPLIANCE AND CONFORMITY

When people are extrinsically motivated, they may adhere to expectations or conform to norms. The desire to gain rewards or avoid punishment can influence our behavior, even if it may not align with our intrinsic interests or values. For example, a student might study diligently not because they are genuinely interested in the subject matter, but because they want to earn a good grade or avoid parental disapproval. This behavior is driven by external pressures rather than internal motivation.

POTENTIAL LIMITATIONS ON LONG-TERM MOTIVATION

Although extrinsic motivation might produce short-term results, it often fails to foster the kind of sustained engagement and intrinsic satisfaction that is crucial for long-term success and well-being. Relying solely on external rewards may diminish an activity's intrinsic enjoyment and passion over time. A child who initially loves drawing, for instance, may lose interest if parental praise is only given for competition wins. The focus shifts from the joy of creating to the pressure of achieving external validation, potentially extinguishing the intrinsic motivation to draw for its own sake.

Harnessing Intrinsic and Extrinsic Motivation

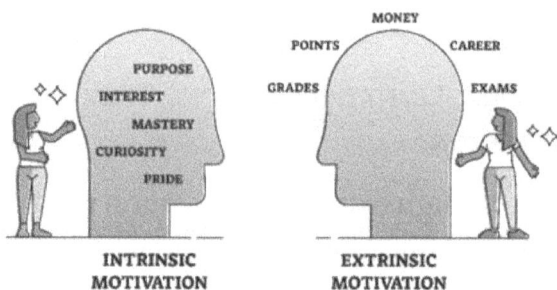

To harness the power of both intrinsic and extrinsic motivation effectively, consider the following strategies.

ALIGN TASKS WITH PERSONAL VALUES AND PASSIONS

Seek opportunities that align with your values, strengths, and interests. For example, if you value creativity and possess strong writing skills, pursuing a career in journalism or content creation would likely resonate with your intrinsic motivations. When tasks resonate with your intrinsic motivations, you are more likely to experience deep engagement and sustained enthusiasm, resulting in higher levels of performance and fulfillment.

SET MEANINGFUL GOALS

Establish clear and meaningful goals that connect with both intrinsic and extrinsic motivators. For example, if your goal is to learn a new programming language (intrinsic motivation: intellectual curiosity and a desire for self-improvement), you could also set a goal of applying that skill to build a portfolio website for freelance work (extrinsic motivation: earning income and building your professional profile). This approach allows you to tap into your intrinsic motivation by aligning your goals with your values and aspirations while acknowledging the potential external rewards or recognition that may accompany your achievements.

FOSTER AUTONOMY AND CHOICE

Whenever possible, seek opportunities to exercise autonomy and have a sense of control over your tasks. When you are given the autonomy to make decisions and mold your work to your liking, it significantly boosts your intrinsic motivation, strengthens your sense of ownership, and increases your overall engagement in the process.

RECOGNIZE AND CELEBRATE PROGRESS

Take time to acknowledge and celebrate your achievements along the way. By recognizing milestones and progress, you reinforce both intrinsic and extrinsic motivation. Positive feedback and self-rewarding practices can fuel your motivation, boost self-confidence, and encourage further effort and progress.

CULTIVATE A SUPPORTIVE ENVIRONMENT

Surround yourself with a supportive network that encourages and values your efforts. Positive social interactions, encouragement from mentors or peers, and recognition from others can provide extrinsic motivation that complements and enhances your intrinsic drive.

SET UP EXTERNAL REWARDS STRATEGICALLY

To maximize the impact of extrinsic motivation, rewards must be implemented strategically. Use them as recognition or reinforcement tools to acknowledge progress or outstanding achievements. Link these rewards to specific milestones or accomplishments to maintain a balance between intrinsic and extrinsic motivation.

CONTINUOUSLY REASSESS AND ALIGN MOTIVATIONS

Regularly assess your motivations to ensure they align with your evolving goals, values, and aspirations. What may have initially been driven by extrinsic factors may develop into a deeper intrinsic motivation over time. For example, you might start a job solely for the high salary (extrinsic motivation). However, as you become more skilled and invested in the work itself, you may find genuine satisfaction and purpose in your contributions (intrinsic motivation), leading you to stay even if a higher-paying opportunity arises elsewhere. Stay attuned to your inner drive and adjust accordingly.

Intrinsic and extrinsic motivation are pivotal in driving our behavior and shaping our journey toward success. By understanding the differences between the two and harnessing their power effectively, we can unlock our full potential and achieve remarkable feats.

Embrace the intrinsic joy and fulfillment of pursuing tasks that align with your passions and values while also recognizing that external rewards and personal passions are the fuel that ignites our motivation, enthusiasm, and drive.

They are the activities, interests, and pursuits that bring us joy, fulfillment, and a deep sense of purpose. Connecting with our passions can unlock our true potential and lead lives infused with meaning and fulfillment.

The Significance of Tapping into Personal Passions

Tapping into personal passions is essential for several reasons. Firstly, it brings joy and fulfillment. Engaging in activities that align with our passions allows us to experience a deep sense of enjoyment, enthusiasm, and satisfaction. When we do what we love, time seems to fly, and we are fully present in the moment, immersed in the experience.

Secondly, tapping into personal passions fuels motivation and drive. Passion provides the intrinsic motivation to overcome challenges, persist through obstacles, and strive for excellence. It is a source of inspiration, propelling us forward with unwavering determination and a thirst for growth and achievement.

Additionally, personal passions lead to a sense of purpose and meaning. When we align our lives with our passions, we feel a profound sense of purpose and connection to something greater than ourselves. Our actions are infused with intention, and we contribute to the world in a way that feels authentic and meaningful.

Strategies for Discovering and Nurturing Personal Passions

Consider these strategies for effectively engaging your personal passions.

REFLECT ON CHILDHOOD INTERESTS

Reflect on the activities, hobbies, or interests that captivated you during your childhood. Childhood experiences often hold clues to our true passions. Consider what made you excited, curious, or engaged. Reconnecting with these early interests can help uncover latent passions.

EXPLORE NEW EXPERIENCES

Step outside your comfort zone and explore new experiences. Be open to trying new activities, hobbies, or subjects that pique your curiosity. By exposing yourself to diverse experiences, you may stumble upon a passion you never knew existed. Stepping outside your comfort zone and exploring new experiences is essential for personal growth and self-discovery. Trying new activities, hobbies, or subjects can broaden your perspective, enhance your creativity, and help you discover hidden talents or passions. Embracing diverse experiences allows you to push your boundaries, break routines, and cultivate a sense of adventure and curiosity in life.

PAY ATTENTION TO WHAT ENERGIZES YOU

Observe how different activities or pursuits make you feel. Pay attention to the activities that energize and uplift you, make you lose track of time, and bring you joy and ful-fillment. These are often indications of your passions. For example, if you notice that spending time in nature, hiking, and taking photographs makes you feel alive and in-spired, these activities may indicate your pas-sions. Pay attention to how these activities make you feel and the joy and fulfillment they bring you.

REFLECT ON CORE VALUES AND BELIEFS

Consider your core values and beliefs. Reflect on the activities or causes that align with those values. Pursuing passions con-gruent with your values creates a sense of alignment, authenticity, and purpose. When you engage in activities that resonate with your core values, a profound sense of pur-pose and authenticity envelops you. Your ac-tions become a manifestation of your beliefs, creating a harmonious alignment between your inner convictions and your external en-deavors. Pursuing passions that align with your values enriches your life and contributes meaningfully to the world around you. This synergy between what you hold dear and what you actively pursue fuels a sense of fulfillment and drives you towards a meaningful and purposeful life.

SEEK INSPIRATION FROM OTHERS

Pursue inspiration from individuals who are passionate about their endeavors. Surround yourself with people who are engaged in activities that resonate with you. Their enthusiasm and dedication can motivate and inspire you as you explore and nurture your passions.

EXPERIMENT AND ITERATE

Embrace a mindset of experimentation and iteration. Try out different activities, projects, or pursuits related to your interests. Don't be afraid to explore multiple avenues to discover the true extent of your passions. Allow yourself the freedom to evolve and refine your understanding of what truly ignites your fire within. For example, if you are interested in art, you could experiment with various mediums such as painting, drawing, sculpting, or digital art. By trying different techniques and styles, you can explore what resonates most with you and where your creative strengths lie. Through this process of experimentation and iteration, you may discover a particular medium that ignites your passion and allows you to express yourself in a unique and fulfilling way.

The Transformative Power of Personal Passion

Tapping into personal passions holds transformative power in various aspects of our lives. Our passions are the driving forces that fuel our desires, dreams, and actions. By harnessing and cultivating our passions, we open a pathway to self-discovery, fulfillment, and growth. Furthermore, pursuing these passions can profoundly impact both our personal and professional lives.

GREATER FULFILLMENT AND HAPPINESS

When we engage in activities that align with our passions, we experience a heightened sense of fulfillment, purpose, and happiness. Life becomes more meaningful and enjoyable as we immerse ourselves in what truly resonates with us.

INCREASED MOTIVATION AND DRIVE

Personal passions provide the fuel that drives us forward. When we are passionate about what we do, we tap into an intrinsic motivation that fuels our determination, resilience, and commitment. We are more likely to overcome obstacles and persevere in facing challenges.

UNLEASHED CREATIVITY AND INNOVATION

Personal passions unleash our creative potential. When deeply engaged in activities we love, our minds are open to new possibilities, and we think outside the box. Passionate individuals often have the ability to innovate, find unique solutions, and make significant contributions in their chosen fields.

ENHANCED PERFORMANCE AND EXCELLENCE

Passionate individuals consistently strive for excellence. They are willing to put in the necessary effort, practice, and continuous improvement to excel in their areas of passion. This commitment to mastery often leads to outstanding performance and the ability to make a significant impact.

INCREASED RESILIENCE AND PERSEVERANCE

Personal passion provides a source of resilience and perseverance. When faced with challenges, setbacks, or failures, our passion fuels us to persist and find alternative paths to success. Passionate individuals view obstacles as opportunities for growth and learning, allowing them to bounce back stronger than before.

Tapping into personal passions is a transformative journey that leads to joy, fulfillment, and a deep sense of purpose. By aligning our lives with our passions, we unlock our true potential and make meaningful contributions to the world. Discovering and nurturing our passions requires self-reflection, exploration, and the courage to step outside our comfort zones. Embrace the power of your passions and let them guide you on a path of growth, success, and a well-lived life.

Cultivating a Supportive Environment: Nurturing Growth and Success

A supportive environment plays a crucial role in maintaining motivation and inspiration. The environment we surround ourselves with affects our personal and professional growth. A supportive environment can provide the encouragement, resources, and positive influence needed to thrive and achieve success. We can create a foundation for growth, resilience, and fulfillment by intentionally fostering a supportive environment.

The Importance of Cultivating a Supportive Environment

Cultivating a supportive environment is essential for several reasons. Firstly, it provides a sense of belonging and acceptance.

We feel valued, understood, and supported when surrounded by individuals who genuinely care about our well-being and success. This sense of belonging creates a safe space to freely express ourselves, take risks, and pursue our goals without fear of judgment or rejection.

Secondly, a supportive environment offers encouragement and motivation. When we face challenges or setbacks, having a network of supportive individuals can provide the motivation, inspiration, and emotional support needed to persevere. They can offer guidance, lend a listening ear, and remind us of our strengths and capabilities during difficult times.

Additionally, a supportive environment fosters personal and professional development. It offers opportunities for collaboration, mentorship, and learning from others. In a supportive environment, we can share ideas, receive constructive feedback, and engage in meaningful conversations that broaden our perspectives and fuel our growth.

Strategies for Cultivating a Supportive Environment

The following strategies should be considered for implementation to build and maintain a strong, supportive environment.

SURROUND YOURSELF WITH POSITIVE INFLUENCES

Surround yourself with individuals who uplift and inspire you. Seek out people who share similar values, goals, and aspirations. Positive influences can provide encouragement, motivation, and constructive feedback that propel you on your journey.

FOSTER OPEN AND HONEST COMMUNICATION

Create a culture of open and honest communication within your environment. Encourage dialogue, active listening, and empathy. When people feel heard and valued, they are more likely to contribute authentically and build deeper connections with others.

BUILD A NETWORK OF MENTORS AND ROLE MODELS

Seek out mentors and role models who can guide and inspire you. These individuals can offer valuable insights, share their experiences, and provide guidance in navigating challenges. A mentor or role model can offer support, accountability, and expertise to help you reach your full potential.

COLLABORATE AND SHARE KNOWLEDGE

Promote collaboration by encouraging knowledge and idea sharing. Collaboration leads to diverse perspectives, collective problem-solving, and the opportunity to learn from one another. Encourage teamwork, value different opinions, and create a safe space for collaboration and innovation.

OFFER SUPPORT AND CELEBRATE SUCCESSES

It is important to be supportive when you see others pursuing their goals and celebrating their achievements. It is important to offer encouragement to others, celebrate the successes that they achieve, and acknowledge the important milestones along their journey. By fostering an environment that celebrates accomplishments, you create a culture of positivity and motivation, inspiring individuals to strive for excellence.

PROVIDE RESOURCES AND OPPORTUNITIES

Offer resources and opportunities for growth and development. This can include providing access to educational materials, training programs, or networking events. Individuals with the tools and opportunities to succeed are likelier to thrive and contribute to a supportive environment.

The Transformative Impact of a Supportive Environment

Creating and maintaining a supportive environment has a powerful and transformative impact on many areas of our lives; from our personal relationships and professional success to everything that shapes our daily life, this positive change is far-reaching and significant.

ENHANCED WELL-BEING AND RESILIENCE

A supportive environment nurtures our well-being and resilience. It provides emotional support during challenging times, reducing stress and promoting a sense of belonging and connection. With a supportive network, we are better equipped to bounce back from setbacks and confidently face future challenges.

INCREASED MOTIVATION AND CONFIDENCE

Supportive individuals can provide the motivation and confidence needed to pursue our goals. They offer encouragement, belief in our abilities, and a sense of validation. This support boosts our self-esteem and belief in our potential, leading to increased motivation and a willingness to take on new challenges.

ACCELERATED LEARNING AND GROWTH

We can access diverse perspectives, experiences, and knowledge in a supportive environment. This accelerates our learning and personal growth as we absorb new information, challenge our assumptions, and expand our horizons. The collective wisdom and support of others can propel us toward new heights of achievement.

EXPANDED NETWORK AND OPPORTUNITIES

A supportive environment connects us with like-minded individuals and expands our network. We gain access to new opportunities, collaborations, and potential partnerships by engaging with a supportive community. This network can open doors to career advancement, personal growth, and meaningful relationships.

GREATER INNOVATION AND CREATIVITY

When individuals feel supported and empowered, they are likelier to think creatively and innovate. Individuals feel safe to share their ideas, take risks, and explore new possibilities. This fosters a culture of innovation and creative problem-solving, leading to breakthroughs and new opportunities.

Cultivating a supportive environment is a powerful catalyst for personal and professional growth. We can thrive and achieve our full potential when surrounded by individuals who genuinely care, offer support, and inspire us. By intentionally fostering a supportive environment, we create a nurturing ecosystem that fuels resilience, motivation, and well-being. Embrace the power of a supportive environment and let it serve as a foundation for growth, collaboration, and success.

Harnessing the Power of Role Models and Mentors: Guiding the Path to Success

Role models and mentors can provide invaluable guidance, wisdom, and inspiration. By harnessing the power of role models and mentors, you will gain insights, learn from their successes and failures, and be inspired to reach greater heights.

It is impossible to overstate just how crucial the guidance and support provided by mentors and role models are to our journey of self-improvement and achievement. Not only have they achieved remarkable feats and possess valuable expertise, but these individuals are also characterized by their willingness to share their knowledge and experiences with others, making them exceptional people. We can navigate our paths with greater clarity, confidence, and purpose by embracing role models' and mentors' wisdom and guidance.

What's the difference between a role model and a mentor? Although both provide direction, role models offer inspiration from a distance, like a guiding light. A mentor, however, walks alongside, offering hands-on support and tailored advice, shaping your journey directly.

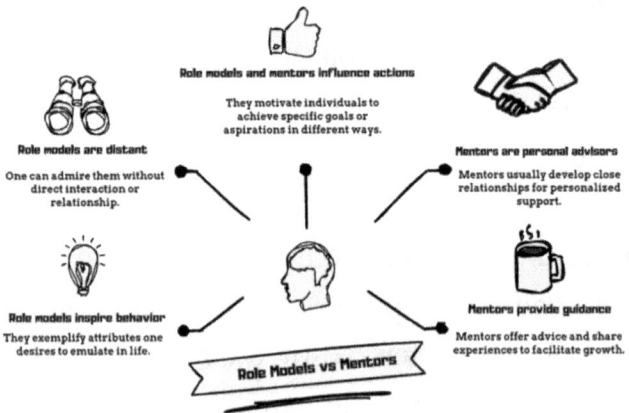

Role models and mentors influence actions

They motivate individuals to achieve specific goals or aspirations in different ways.

Role models are distant

One can admire them without direct interaction or relationship.

Mentors are personal advisors

Mentors usually develop close relationships for personalized support.

Role models inspire behavior

They exemplify attributes one desires to emulate in life.

Mentors provide guidance

Mentors offer advice and share experiences to facilitate growth.

Role Models vs Mentors

The Significance of Role Models and Mentors

Role models and mentors profoundly impact our personal and professional development for several reasons. They provide inspiration and aspiration and exemplify the qualities, values, and achievements we strive to emulate. They demonstrate what is possible and ignite our ambition, inspiring us to set higher goals and reach new heights.

Role models and mentors offer guidance and wisdom. Their experiences and expertise provide valuable insights into navigating challenges, making decisions, and seizing opportunities. They have traversed the path we aspire to embark upon, and their guidance can help us avoid pitfalls and accelerate our progress.

Additionally, mentors provide emotional support and encouragement. They believe in our potential, offer constructive feedback, and provide a safe space for us to share our fears, doubts, and aspirations. Their presence and guidance instill confidence, nurture resilience, and reinforce our belief in ourselves.

Benefits of Harnessing Role Models and Mentors

Harnessing the power of role models and mentors brings numerous benefits to our personal and professional lives.

KNOWLEDGE AND EXPERTISE

Role models and mentors have valuable knowledge and expertise in their respective fields. Their guidance allows us to tap into their wisdom, learn from their experiences, and gain insights that would take us years to acquire on our own. This accelerates our learning and growth, saving us from unnecessary detours and mistakes.

EXPANDED PERSPECTIVES

Role models and mentors offer different perspectives, broadening our horizons and challenging our assumptions. They expose us to new ideas, approaches, and possibilities, helping us see beyond our limitations. This expanded perspective enhances our creativity, problem-solving skills, and innovation ability.

NETWORKING AND OPPORTUNITIES

Role models and mentors provide access to valuable networks and opportunities. Their connections and influence can open doors to new collaborations, partnerships, and career opportunities. Their guidance and endorsement can enhance our credibility and visibility within our respective fields.

EMOTIONAL SUPPORT AND MOTIVATION

Role models and mentors provide emotional support, encouragement, and motivation. They offer a listening ear, lend their wisdom during challenging times, and provide the reassurance needed to persevere in adversity. Their belief in our potential and consistent support fuels our motivation and resilience.

Strategies for Finding and Leveraging Role Models and Mentors

To effectively utilize the guidance and inspiration provided by role models and mentors, consider implementing the following strategic approaches for optimal results and personal growth.

DEFINE YOUR GOALS AND ASPIRATIONS

Clarify your goals AND aspirations to identify the areas where you would benefit from the guidance of a role model or mentor. Determine the specific skills, knowledge, or experiences you seek to acquire. For example, if your goal is to become a successful entrepreneur, you might identify a need for mentorship in areas like securing funding, building a strong team, or developing a robust business plan. You could then seek out a mentor with experience in these specific areas.

SEEK INSPIRATION FROM DIVERSE SOURCES

Seek motivation from individuals who exhibit attributes and accomplishments that you hold in high regard, even if their expertise does not directly align with your area of interest. This widens your perspective and exposes you to a broader range of possibilities. For example, an aspiring entrepreneur might find inspiration in the unwavering dedication of a renowned marathon runner, learning valuable lessons about perseverance and discipline that translate across domains, even though running and business are seemingly unrelated fields.

UTILIZE ONLINE PLATFORMS AND NETWORKS

Explore online platforms, forums, and professional networks to connect with potential role models and mentors such as, LinkedIn, industry-specific forums, and virtual communities provide opportunities to engage with individuals with similar interests or expertise.

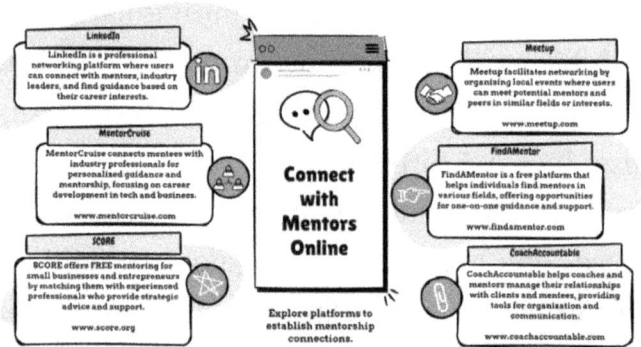

Connect with Mentors Online

Explore platforms to establish mentorship connections.

ENGAGE IN NETWORKING EVENTS AND CONFERENCES

Attend networking events, conferences, and seminars relevant to your field. These events offer opportunities to meet accomplished individuals and establish connections. Approach potential role models or mentors respectfully, expressing your admiration and interest in learning from them.

APPROACH POTENTIAL MENTORS WITH A CLEAR ASK

When approaching a potential mentor, be clear about what you hope to gain from the relationship. Demonstrate your commitment, curiosity, and willingness to learn. Respect their time and expertise, and express gratitude for their guidance.

BUILD GENUINE RELATIONSHIP

Develop authentic relationships with role models and mentors. Show genuine interest in their experiences, achievements, and insights. Demonstrate your eagerness to learn and grow. Building a strong relationship based on trust, respect, and mutual admiration lays the foundation for effective mentorship.

PAY IT FORWARD

As you progress in your journey, consider becoming a role model or mentor to others. Share your knowledge, experiences, and insights with those who seek guidance. By giving back and supporting others on their paths, you contribute to the cycle of learning and growth.

The Transformative Impact of Role Models and Mentors

Harnessing the power of role models and mentors has transformative effects on various aspects of our lives.

PERSONAL AND PROFESSIONAL GROWTH

Role models and mentors accelerate our personal and professional growth by providing guidance, knowledge, and perspective. Their influence propels us forward, enabling us to reach new levels of achievement and fulfillment.

CONFIDENCE AND SELF-BELIEF

Their support and their guidance work together to build our self-esteem, help us conquer self-doubt, and give us the confidence to take on new challenges.

RESILIENCE AND ADAPTABILITY

Through their guidance, we learn to navigate obstacles, persevere despite setbacks, and adapt to changing circumstances. This resilience allows us to bounce back stronger and remain agile in pursuing our goals.

PERSONAL AND PROFESSIONAL NETWORK

Role models and mentors introduce us to valuable networks and connections. We expand our network by leveraging their relationships and introductions, opening doors to new opportunities, collaborations, and partnerships.

LEGACY AND IMPACT

By emulating the achievements and values of role models, we contribute to their legacy and extend their impact. As we grow and achieve success, we become role models for others, paying forward the guidance and support we have received. Harnessing the power of role models and mentors is a transformative endeavor that propels us toward growth, achievement, and personal fulfill-ment.

We can navigate our paths with greater clarity, confidence, and purpose by seeking and leveraging the guidance and wisdom of those who have achieved remarkable feats. Role models and mentors provide invaluable support, knowledge, and inspiration as we pursue our goals and aspirations. Embrace the wisdom and guidance they offer, build authentic relationships, and pay it forward by becoming a role model or mentor to others. Let the power of role models and mentors guide your path to success, and experience the transformative impact it brings to your life and endeavors.

Remember that motivation is not con-stant; it requires ongoing nurturing and re-newal. Motivation and inspiration are the fuel that keeps you moving forward on your path to success. By harnessing intrinsic and extrinsic motivation, tapping into personal passions, cultivating a supportive environment, and harnessing the power of role models and mentors, you will sustain your drive, remain focused, and overcome challenges. Embrace these strategies, seek inspiration from within and outside yourself, and let motivation propel you toward achieving your goals and aspirations.

About the Author

Mario Harris, a retired disabled Marine veteran with over 27 years of service to his country, hails from Mobile, Alabama. He is the eldest son of LeBaron Horace and Nora Harris. After retiring from the Marine Corps, Mario established MENAC (Mentor Every Neighborhood and Community), Inc., a nonprofit organization dedicated to mentoring and supporting single-parent mothers in raising their young men and women while addressing father absenteeism.

Mario graduated from Campbell University in Buies Creek, NC, with a Bachelor of Business Administration. Mario is a respected mentor, speaker, proficient trainer, and consultant in leadership and management. He possesses the ability to inspire and guide both youth and adults toward achieving their desired success.

Mario is married to his wonderful wife, Patricia, and they are proud parents to three children: JaVon, JaMario, and Arianna. Moreover, he cherishes the joy of having one granddaughter named Ja'Naisja. He is also the godparent of Moses, Juwell, and Amina.

Series Bibliography

Adams, S. (2018). The Power of Vision: How to Create a Compelling Vision for Your Life and Business. Adams Media.

Brown, B. (2010). The Gifts of Imperfection: Let Go of Who You Think You're Supposed to Be and Embrace Who You Are. Hazelden Publishing.

Covey, S. R. (2004). The 7 Habits of Highly Effective People: Powerful Lessons in Personal Change. Simon & Schuster.

Dweck, C. S. (2006). Mindset: The New Psychology of Success. Ballantine Books.

Grant, A. M. (2019). Dare to Lead: Brave Work. Tough Conversations. Whole Hearts. Random House.

Hill, N. (2015). Think and Grow Rich. Ballantine Books.

Johnson, S. (2017). Tribes: We Need You to Lead Us. Portfolio.

Kotter, J. P. (2012). Leading Change. Harvard Business Review Press.

Meyer, P. (2017). The Power of Habit: Why We Do What We Do in Life and Business. Random House.

Pink, D. H. (2011). Drive: The Surprising Truth About What Motivates Us. Riverhead Books.

Sinek, S. (2009). Start with Why: How Great Leaders Inspire Everyone to Take Action. Portfolio.

Tracy, B. (2017). Eat That Frog!: 21 Great Ways to Stop Procrastinating and Get More Done in Less Time. Berrett-Koehler Publishers.

Vaden, R. (2015). Procrastinate on Purpose: 5 Permissions to Multiply Your Time. Penguin Random House.

Note: This bibliography includes books that may provide further insights and resources on the topics covered in The Goal Achiever's Blueprint: Unlocking the 7 Key Traits for Success. The list is not exhaustive and should be adapted to suit individual reading preferences and research requirements.

www.ingramcontent.com/pod-product-compliance
Lightning Source LLC
Chambersburg PA
CBHW071638040426
42452CB00009B/1687